I0016987

Table of Contents

Chapter 1: Introduction to AI Applications in Construction

Overview of Artificial Intelligence

Artificial Intelligence (AI) is revolutionizing the construction industry by streamlining processes, enhancing safety, improving project management, and increasing efficiency. In this subchapter, we will provide an overview of AI applications in construction, covering various aspects such as safety, project management, materials management, scheduling, quality control, cost estimation, equipment monitoring, risk assessment, sustainable construction practices, and site optimization. This guide is designed for individuals who want to delve deeper into the world of AI applications in construction and understand how this technology is transforming the industry.

AI applications in construction safety are helping to prevent accidents and save lives by using predictive analytics to identify potential hazards on construction sites. By analyzing data from sensors and cameras, AI can detect unsafe conditions and alert workers in real-time, reducing the risk of accidents. Additionally, AI-powered drones and robots can be used to conduct safety inspections, eliminating the need for workers to enter dangerous areas.

In terms of project management, AI is being used to optimize schedules, allocate resources efficiently, and monitor progress in real-time. Project managers can use AI algorithms to predict potential delays, identify bottlenecks, and make informed decisions to keep projects on track. AI can also help with cost estimation by analyzing historical data, material costs, and labor rates to provide accurate and reliable estimates for construction projects.

Materials management is another area where AI is making a significant impact in the construction industry. By using AI-powered software, construction companies can track inventory, predict material shortages, and optimize procurement processes. This not only reduces waste and saves time but also ensures that projects are completed on time and within budget.

AI applications in construction scheduling are helping to optimize workflows, reduce downtime, and improve productivity. By using AI algorithms to analyze data and predict future trends, construction companies can create more efficient schedules that minimize delays and maximize resource utilization. This results in faster project completion times and higher profitability for construction companies.

In conclusion, AI applications in construction are transforming the industry by enhancing safety, improving project management, streamlining materials management, optimizing scheduling, and reducing costs. By leveraging the power of AI technology, construction companies can increase efficiency, productivity, and profitability while ensuring that projects are completed on time and within budget. This subchapter provides a comprehensive overview of AI applications in construction, covering various aspects that are crucial for individuals looking to learn more about this exciting field.

Importance of AI in the Construction Industry

Artificial Intelligence (AI) has become increasingly important in the construction industry, revolutionizing the way projects are planned, managed, and executed. From safety to project management, materials management to scheduling, quality control to cost estimation, AI is transforming every aspect of construction. This subchapter will delve into the significance of AI in the construction industry, highlighting its benefits and potential applications.

In terms of safety, AI plays a crucial role in identifying potential hazards on construction sites and preventing accidents before they occur. By utilizing advanced algorithms and machine learning techniques, AI can analyze data from sensors and cameras to detect unsafe conditions and alert workers in real-time. This proactive approach to safety not only saves lives but also minimizes project delays and costly accidents.

In project management, AI tools can streamline workflows, optimize resource allocation, and improve overall efficiency. By analyzing historical data and predicting future trends, AI algorithms can help project managers make informed decisions and mitigate risks. From prioritizing tasks to tracking progress, AI applications in project management can significantly improve project outcomes and deliverables.

Materials management is another area where AI is making a significant impact in the construction industry. By optimizing inventory levels, predicting material shortages, and identifying cost-saving opportunities, AI can help construction companies reduce waste, lower costs, and improve overall supply chain efficiency. With AI-powered systems in place, construction companies can better manage their materials and ensure timely delivery to the job site.

Scheduling is a critical aspect of construction projects, and AI can help optimize schedules, reduce delays, and improve project timelines. By analyzing historical data, weather patterns, and resource availability, AI algorithms can generate more accurate schedules and identify potential bottlenecks before they occur. This proactive approach to scheduling can lead to smoother project execution and better overall project outcomes.

In conclusion, the importance of AI in the construction industry cannot be overstated. From safety to project management, materials management to scheduling, AI applications are transforming every aspect of construction. By leveraging AI technologies, construction companies can improve efficiency, reduce costs, and enhance overall project outcomes. For anyone looking to learn more about AI applications in construction, this subchapter provides a comprehensive guide to the benefits and potential applications of AI in the construction industry.

Benefits of Using AI in Construction Projects

AI technology has revolutionized the construction industry in recent years, offering a wide range of benefits for construction projects. One of the key advantages of using AI in construction projects is improved efficiency. AI algorithms can analyze vast amounts of data quickly and accurately, allowing construction teams to make more informed decisions and streamline processes. This can lead to significant time and cost savings, as well as increased productivity on the job site.

Another benefit of using AI in construction projects is enhanced safety. AI-powered sensors and drones can monitor job sites in real-time, identifying potential hazards and alerting workers to potential dangers. This can help prevent accidents and injuries, making construction sites safer for workers and reducing the risk of costly delays or shutdowns due to accidents.

AI technology can also improve project management in construction projects. AI algorithms can analyze project data and identify potential issues before they become problems, allowing project managers to proactively address issues and keep projects on track. This can help ensure that construction projects are completed on time and within budget, leading to greater overall success for construction teams.

In addition, AI technology can be used to optimize construction materials management. AI algorithms can analyze data on materials usage and predict future needs, helping construction teams to better plan and manage their materials inventory. This can reduce waste and minimize the risk of running out of essential materials during a project, leading to smoother construction processes and improved project outcomes.

Overall, the use of AI in construction projects offers a range of benefits, from improved efficiency and safety to enhanced project management and materials management. By harnessing the power of AI technology, construction teams can achieve greater success on their projects and stay ahead of the competition in an increasingly complex and competitive industry.

Chapter 2: AI Applications in Construction Safety

AI Technologies for Enhancing Safety on Construction Sites

AI technologies are revolutionizing the construction industry by enhancing safety on construction sites. These technologies utilize advanced algorithms and machine learning to predict and prevent potential hazards, ultimately reducing the risk of accidents and injuries. By implementing AI applications in construction safety, project managers and site supervisors can proactively identify safety issues and take corrective actions to ensure a safe working environment for all workers.

One of the key AI technologies for enhancing safety on construction sites is the use of predictive analytics. By analyzing historical data and real-time information, AI algorithms can identify patterns and trends that indicate potential safety risks. For example, AI can analyze data from sensors and cameras to detect unsafe behaviors or conditions, such as workers not wearing proper safety gear or equipment malfunctions. By predicting these risks in advance, construction companies can implement preventive measures to mitigate the dangers and prevent accidents from happening.

Another important AI application in construction safety is the use of computer vision technology. This technology enables construction sites to use cameras and drones to monitor and analyze activities in real-time. By using computer vision algorithms, AI can identify potential safety hazards, such as workers in dangerous areas or equipment operating in unsafe conditions. This allows site supervisors to take immediate action to address the issues and prevent accidents before they occur.

Furthermore, AI technologies can also be used in safety training and education programs for construction workers. By using virtual reality simulations and interactive training modules, AI can provide workers with hands-on experience in identifying and responding to safety hazards. This not only improves safety awareness among workers but also helps them develop the skills and knowledge needed to prevent accidents on the construction site.

In conclusion, AI technologies offer a wide range of applications for enhancing safety on construction sites. By leveraging predictive analytics, computer vision, and virtual reality, construction companies can proactively identify and address safety risks, ultimately creating a safer working environment for all workers. As the construction industry continues to adopt AI technologies, the importance of prioritizing safety on construction sites will become even more crucial in ensuring the well-being of workers and the successful completion of projects.

Predictive Analytics for Accident Prevention

Predictive analytics is a powerful tool in accident prevention within the construction industry. By analyzing historical data and trends, AI applications can identify potential risks and hazards before they lead to accidents on construction sites. This proactive approach allows for targeted interventions and safety measures to be implemented, ultimately reducing the likelihood of accidents occurring.

One of the key benefits of using predictive analytics for accident prevention is the ability to prioritize safety efforts based on data-driven insights. By focusing on the most high-risk areas and activities, construction companies can allocate resources more effectively and efficiently to prevent accidents before they happen. This targeted approach can help save lives, reduce injuries, and minimize costly downtime on construction projects.

AI applications in construction safety can also help improve communication and coordination among workers on site. By analyzing real-time data from sensors and wearable devices, predictive analytics can alert workers and supervisors to potential safety hazards in the environment. This timely information can enable quick response and intervention to prevent accidents from occurring, fostering a culture of safety and vigilance on construction sites.

In addition to preventing accidents, predictive analytics can also help improve overall project management in construction. By forecasting potential delays or bottlenecks in the construction process, AI applications can help project managers make informed decisions to keep projects on track and on budget. This predictive capability can lead to more efficient project delivery and higher client satisfaction, ultimately benefiting both construction companies and their clients.

Overall, predictive analytics for accident prevention is a valuable tool in the construction industry, offering numerous benefits in terms of safety, project management, and overall project success. By harnessing the power of AI applications, construction companies can proactively identify and mitigate risks, leading to safer worksites, more efficient project delivery, and ultimately, a more successful construction operation.

Real-time Monitoring of Safety Compliance Using AI

Real-time monitoring of safety compliance is a crucial aspect of construction projects, as it ensures the well-being of workers and prevents accidents on site. With the advancement of technology, Artificial Intelligence (AI) has become an indispensable tool in achieving this goal. AI applications in construction have revolutionized the way safety compliance is monitored, providing real-time insights and alerts to prevent potential hazards.

Using AI algorithms, construction companies can now track safety compliance in real-time, analyzing data from various sources such as wearable devices, CCTV cameras, and sensors placed on equipment and machinery. These AI systems can detect unsafe behaviors or conditions, alerting supervisors and workers immediately to take corrective actions. This proactive approach helps prevent accidents before they occur, ultimately saving lives and reducing the risk of costly delays.

AI applications in construction safety not only monitor compliance but also provide valuable insights for future safety improvements. By analyzing historical data and trends, AI systems can identify patterns that may lead to accidents and suggest preventive measures. This data-driven approach enables construction companies to continuously improve their safety protocols, creating a safer working environment for all employees.

In addition to monitoring safety compliance, AI can also assist in predicting potential risks on construction sites. By analyzing data from past projects and current conditions, AI algorithms can identify potential hazards and assess the likelihood of accidents occurring. This predictive capability allows construction companies to take proactive measures to mitigate risks and ensure the safety of all workers on site.

Overall, real-time monitoring of safety compliance using AI is a game-changer in the construction industry, providing valuable insights, proactive alerts, and predictive capabilities to prevent accidents and ensure the well-being of workers. As construction projects become more complex and demanding, AI applications in safety compliance will continue to play a vital role in creating a safer and more efficient work environment.

Chapter 3: AI Applications in Construction Project Management

Automation of Project Planning and Scheduling

In the field of construction, project planning and scheduling are critical components that can make or break the success of a project. With the advancement of technology, particularly in the field of artificial intelligence (AI), automation of project planning and scheduling has become increasingly popular. This subchapter will delve into the various AI applications in construction that can streamline and optimize project planning and scheduling processes.

One of the key advantages of using AI in project planning and scheduling is the ability to analyze vast amounts of data quickly and accurately. AI algorithms can process historical project data, current market trends, and other relevant information to generate more accurate project schedules. This not only saves time but also improves the overall efficiency of the planning process.

Another benefit of using AI in project planning and scheduling is the ability to identify potential risks and issues before they arise. AI algorithms can analyze project data to predict potential delays, cost overruns, and other risks that may impact the project timeline. By identifying these risks early on, project managers can take proactive measures to mitigate them and keep the project on track.

AI applications in construction project management also play a crucial role in optimizing resource allocation. By analyzing project data and resource availability, AI algorithms can recommend the most efficient allocation of resources to maximize productivity and minimize costs. This ensures that projects are completed on time and within budget.

Furthermore, AI can also be used to automate the generation of project schedules and timelines. By inputting project requirements and constraints into AI algorithms, project managers can quickly generate detailed project schedules that take into account all relevant factors. This not only saves time but also ensures that project schedules are accurate and realistic.

Overall, the automation of project planning and scheduling through AI applications in construction offers numerous benefits, including improved accuracy, risk identification, resource optimization, and time savings. By leveraging AI technology in these areas, construction companies can streamline their project management processes and achieve better outcomes for their projects.

AI Tools for Resource Allocation and Optimization

AI tools are revolutionizing the way resources are allocated and optimized in the construction industry. These tools utilize advanced algorithms and machine learning techniques to analyze data and make informed decisions that can lead to more efficient resource management. By incorporating AI into resource allocation processes, construction companies can streamline their operations, reduce costs, and improve overall project outcomes.

One key area where AI tools are making a significant impact is in construction project management. These tools can analyze project data in real-time, identify potential bottlenecks or issues, and suggest solutions to optimize resource allocation. By leveraging AI, project managers can make more informed decisions that lead to better project timelines, budget adherence, and overall success.

In addition to project management, AI tools are also being used to optimize materials management in construction. By analyzing historical data, current inventory levels, and project requirements, AI can help companies determine the most cost-effective and efficient way to procure, store, and use materials. This can result in reduced waste, lower costs, and improved project efficiency.

Another area where AI tools are proving to be invaluable is in construction scheduling. By analyzing project schedules, resource availability, and potential risks, AI can help companies create more accurate and realistic project timelines. This can lead to better resource allocation, improved productivity, and reduced delays on construction projects.

Overall, AI tools for resource allocation and optimization are transforming the construction industry by providing companies with the tools they need to make more informed decisions, streamline operations, and improve project outcomes. By incorporating AI into various aspects of construction, companies can increase efficiency, reduce costs, and ultimately deliver better results for their clients.

Risk Assessment and Mitigation Strategies with AI

Risk assessment is a crucial aspect of construction projects, as it helps identify potential hazards and uncertainties that could impact the project's success. With the advancement of technology, artificial intelligence (AI) has emerged as a powerful tool in mitigating risks in construction projects. By leveraging AI applications, construction professionals can enhance their risk assessment processes and develop effective mitigation strategies to ensure project success.

One of the key benefits of using AI in risk assessment is its ability to analyze vast amounts of data quickly and accurately. AI algorithms can process data from various sources, such as historical project data, environmental factors, and real-time sensor data, to identify potential risks and predict their likelihood of occurrence. This enables construction professionals to make informed decisions and take proactive measures to mitigate risks before they escalate into larger issues.

AI applications in construction also offer innovative solutions for risk mitigation strategies. For example, AI-powered predictive analytics can forecast potential risks based on historical data and ongoing project conditions. This allows project managers to implement preventive measures and adjust project plans to minimize the impact of potential risks. Additionally, AI can automate risk assessment processes, saving time and resources while ensuring thorough analysis of all potential risks.

In addition to risk assessment, AI can also assist in identifying vulnerabilities in construction projects and developing robust mitigation strategies. By analyzing project data and identifying patterns or anomalies, AI can uncover potential weak points in the project plan or execution.

This allows construction professionals to address vulnerabilities proactively and implement measures to strengthen project resilience.

Overall, AI applications in risk assessment and mitigation strategies offer construction professionals a powerful tool to enhance project success and minimize uncertainties. By leveraging AI technologies, construction projects can benefit from improved risk assessment processes, proactive risk mitigation strategies, and enhanced project resilience. As AI continues to evolve, its role in construction risk management will only become more significant, paving the way for safer, more efficient, and successful construction projects.

Chapter 4: AI Applications in Construction Materials Management

Inventory Management with AI

Inventory management is a crucial aspect of any construction project, as it involves tracking and controlling the flow of materials and supplies needed for the job. With the advancement of technology, Artificial Intelligence (AI) has become a game-changer in the construction industry, particularly in the realm of inventory management. AI applications in construction have revolutionized the way materials are monitored, tracked, and managed throughout a project.

One of the key benefits of using AI in inventory management is its ability to predict material requirements accurately. By analyzing historical data and project specifications, AI algorithms can forecast the quantity and type of materials needed at each stage of the construction process. This predictive capability helps project managers avoid stockouts, reduce waste, and optimize inventory levels, ultimately leading to cost savings and improved project efficiency.

AI applications in inventory management also enhance visibility and transparency across the supply chain. By integrating AI-powered systems with inventory management software, construction companies can track the movement of materials in real-time, monitor stock levels, and identify potential bottlenecks or delays. This real-time data allows project managers to make informed decisions quickly, ensuring that materials are delivered to the right place at the right time.

Furthermore, AI can automate routine inventory management tasks, such as reordering supplies, updating inventory records, and conducting physical inventory counts. By delegating these repetitive tasks to AI systems, construction companies can free up valuable time for their employees to focus on more strategic activities. This automation not only improves operational efficiency but also reduces the risk of human error in inventory management processes.

In conclusion, AI applications in inventory management have the potential to transform the construction industry by streamlining operations, reducing costs, and improving project outcomes. By harnessing the power of AI algorithms to predict material requirements, enhance visibility across the supply chain, and automate routine tasks, construction companies can optimize their inventory management practices and stay ahead of the competition. As AI technology continues to evolve, we can expect to see even more innovative solutions that revolutionize the way materials are managed in construction projects.

Supply Chain Optimization Using Artificial Intelligence

Supply chain management is a critical aspect of the construction industry, ensuring that materials, equipment, and resources are delivered to the right place at the right time. With the advent of artificial intelligence (AI), supply chain optimization has become more efficient and effective than ever before. AI applications in construction have revolutionized the way companies manage their supply chains, streamlining processes and reducing costs.

One of the key benefits of using AI in supply chain optimization is its ability to analyze vast amounts of data quickly and accurately. AI algorithms can predict demand, identify potential bottlenecks, and optimize delivery schedules to ensure materials are available when needed. This predictive capability helps construction companies avoid delays and costly downtime, improving overall project efficiency.

AI applications in construction materials management have also proven to be invaluable in optimizing supply chains. By analyzing historical data and trends, AI systems can recommend the most cost-effective suppliers, monitor inventory levels, and even automate reordering processes. This level of automation not only saves time but also reduces the risk of human error, ensuring that projects stay on track and within budget.

In addition to materials management, AI can also be used to optimize equipment monitoring in construction projects. By installing sensors and IoT devices on machinery, AI systems can track performance, predict maintenance needs, and even detect potential issues before they arise. This proactive approach to equipment monitoring helps prevent costly breakdowns and ensures that projects run smoothly from start to finish.

Overall, AI applications in supply chain optimization have transformed the construction industry, making processes more efficient, cost-effective, and reliable. By harnessing the power of AI algorithms, construction companies can streamline their supply chains, improve project timelines, and ultimately deliver better results for their clients. As technology continues to advance, the role of AI in construction will only become more prominent, shaping the future of the industry for years to come.

Quality Control in Material Selection and Procurement

Quality control in material selection and procurement is a crucial aspect of ensuring the success of any construction project. With the advancements in artificial intelligence (AI) technology, construction companies now have powerful tools at their disposal to streamline and improve this process. In this subchapter, we will delve into how AI applications can revolutionize material selection and procurement in construction.

One of the key benefits of using AI in material selection and procurement is the ability to analyze vast amounts of data quickly and accurately. AI algorithms can process data from various sources, such as supplier databases, material specifications, and project requirements, to identify the best materials for a given project. This not only saves time but also helps to ensure that the materials selected meet the required quality standards.

Furthermore, AI applications can help construction companies optimize their procurement processes by identifying the most cost-effective suppliers and negotiating better deals. By analyzing historical data and market trends, AI algorithms can predict future price fluctuations and help companies make informed decisions about when and where to purchase materials. This can result in significant cost savings for construction projects.

In addition to cost savings, AI can also improve the quality of materials used in construction projects. By analyzing the performance of different materials in various conditions, AI algorithms can recommend the most suitable materials for a specific project based on factors such as durability, strength, and environmental impact. This ensures that the materials selected meet the highest quality standards and contribute to the overall success of the project.

Overall, AI applications in material selection and procurement have the potential to revolutionize the construction industry by improving efficiency, reducing costs, and enhancing the quality of construction projects. By leveraging the power of AI technology, construction companies can stay ahead of the competition, deliver projects more effectively, and ultimately achieve greater success in the long run. As technology continues to advance, the possibilities for AI applications in construction are endless, making it an exciting time to explore the potential of AI in material selection and procurement.

Chapter 5: AI Applications in Construction Scheduling

AI-driven Scheduling Algorithms

AI-driven scheduling algorithms are revolutionizing the construction industry by streamlining the project planning process and optimizing resource allocation. These algorithms leverage artificial intelligence to analyze vast amounts of data and make real-time adjustments to construction schedules, resulting in increased efficiency and reduced project delays. By incorporating AI into scheduling practices, construction companies can achieve greater accuracy, reliability, and flexibility in project management.

One of the key benefits of AI-driven scheduling algorithms is their ability to adapt to changing project conditions. Traditional scheduling methods often struggle to account for unexpected delays or resource constraints, leading to costly disruptions and project overruns. AI algorithms, on the other hand, can quickly reevaluate schedules based on new information and make proactive adjustments to minimize the impact of disruptions. This dynamic approach to scheduling allows construction companies to respond swiftly to changing circumstances and maintain project timelines.

AI-driven scheduling algorithms also offer enhanced predictive capabilities, allowing construction companies to forecast project timelines more accurately. By analyzing historical data, current project status, and external factors such as weather conditions and material availability, AI algorithms can generate more reliable estimates of project completion dates. This increased accuracy in scheduling predictions enables construction companies to better manage project risks and allocate resources more effectively, ultimately leading to improved project outcomes.

Furthermore, AI-driven scheduling algorithms can optimize resource allocation by identifying inefficiencies and bottlenecks in construction workflows. By analyzing data on workforce availability, equipment utilization, and material deliveries, AI algorithms can identify opportunities to streamline operations and reduce wastage. This proactive approach to resource management not only improves project efficiency but also helps construction companies minimize costs and maximize productivity.

In conclusion, AI-driven scheduling algorithms are transforming the construction industry by providing advanced tools for project planning and resource management. By harnessing the power of artificial intelligence, construction companies can achieve greater efficiency, accuracy, and flexibility in their scheduling practices. As AI technology continues to evolve, the potential for further innovation in construction scheduling is vast, offering exciting opportunities for improving project outcomes and driving industry growth.

Real-time Updates and Adjustments in Project Timelines

Real-time updates and adjustments in project timelines play a crucial role in the successful implementation of AI applications in construction. With the rapid advancements in technology, project timelines can now be monitored and adjusted in real-time to ensure that construction projects stay on track and within budget. This subchapter will delve into the importance of real-time updates and adjustments in project timelines and how AI can be leveraged to optimize construction processes.

One of the key benefits of real-time updates in project timelines is the ability to quickly identify any potential delays or issues that may arise during the construction process. By utilizing AI applications, project managers can receive instant notifications when a project is falling behind schedule, allowing them to take proactive measures to address the issue before it escalates. This real-time monitoring ensures that construction projects are completed on time and within budget, ultimately leading to greater efficiency and cost savings.

Additionally, real-time updates in project timelines enable construction teams to make informed decisions based on up-to-date information. AI applications can analyze data from various sources, such as weather forecasts, traffic conditions, and material availability, to provide accurate predictions on project timelines. By having access to this real-time data, project managers can adjust schedules, allocate resources more effectively, and mitigate potential risks, ultimately improving project outcomes.

Furthermore, real-time updates in project timelines allow for increased collaboration and communication among project stakeholders. With AI applications, project managers can share real-time updates with team members, subcontractors, and clients, ensuring that everyone is on the same page regarding project progress and timelines. This transparency fosters a collaborative work environment and helps to build trust among stakeholders, leading to smoother project execution and successful outcomes.

In conclusion, real-time updates and adjustments in project timelines are essential components of AI applications in construction. By leveraging AI technology to monitor and adjust project timelines in real-time, construction teams can optimize processes, improve communication, and ultimately achieve project success. As AI continues to revolutionize the construction industry, incorporating real-time updates in project timelines will become standard practice for those looking to stay ahead of the curve in construction project management.

Improving Efficiency and Productivity through AI Scheduling

In the construction industry, efficiency and productivity are crucial factors that can make or break a project. With the help of artificial intelligence (AI) scheduling tools, construction companies can optimize their project timelines and resources to achieve maximum efficiency. AI scheduling involves using algorithms to analyze data and make decisions about how to best allocate resources, manage timelines, and minimize disruptions. By implementing AI scheduling solutions, construction companies can streamline their operations, reduce costs, and improve overall project outcomes.

One of the key benefits of AI scheduling in construction is its ability to optimize project timelines. AI algorithms can analyze historical data, current project status, and external factors such as weather conditions or material availability to predict potential delays and proactively adjust scheduling to avoid them. By using AI scheduling tools, construction companies can create more realistic and achievable project timelines, leading to improved efficiency and on-time project delivery.

Another advantage of AI scheduling in construction is its ability to allocate resources more effectively. AI algorithms can analyze project requirements, resource availability, and constraints to optimize resource allocation and avoid bottlenecks. By using AI scheduling tools, construction companies can ensure that resources are used efficiently and effectively, leading to cost savings and improved productivity.

AI scheduling tools can also help construction companies minimize disruptions and delays by identifying potential issues before they occur. By analyzing data in real-time and predicting potential risks, AI algorithms can help construction companies proactively address issues and make adjustments to prevent delays. This proactive approach can help construction companies avoid costly delays and keep projects on track.

Overall, AI scheduling is a powerful tool that can help construction companies improve efficiency, productivity, and project outcomes. By leveraging AI algorithms to optimize project timelines, allocate resources effectively, and proactively address potential issues, construction companies can streamline their operations, reduce costs, and deliver projects on time and within budget. As AI technology continues to advance, the opportunities for using AI scheduling in construction will only grow, making it an essential tool for companies looking to stay competitive in the industry.

Chapter 6: AI Applications in Construction Quality Control

Automated Inspection and Defect Detection

Automated inspection and defect detection are crucial components of AI applications in construction. By utilizing AI technology, construction companies can streamline their inspection processes and ensure that potential defects are caught early on, saving time and money in the long run. This subchapter will delve into the various ways in which AI is being used to revolutionize inspection and defect detection in the construction industry.

One of the key benefits of automated inspection and defect detection is the ability to identify potential issues before they escalate into larger problems. Through the use of AI-powered drones and cameras, construction companies can conduct thorough inspections of their sites without the need for human intervention. This not only saves time but also ensures that no area goes unchecked, leading to a more comprehensive evaluation of the site's condition.

AI applications in construction also allow for real-time defect detection, enabling construction teams to address issues as soon as they arise. By using machine learning algorithms to analyze data from sensors and cameras, AI can quickly identify anomalies and alert project managers to potential defects. This proactive approach to defect detection helps to minimize delays and costly rework, ultimately improving project efficiency.

Furthermore, AI can be used to automate the documentation of defects, making it easier for construction teams to track and manage issues throughout the project lifecycle. By digitally capturing and storing information about defects, project managers can easily reference past issues and monitor trends over time. This data-driven approach to defect detection not only improves the overall quality of construction projects but also provides valuable insights for future planning and decision-making.

In conclusion, automated inspection and defect detection are essential tools for modern construction companies looking to improve their efficiency and quality control processes. By harnessing the power of AI, construction teams can conduct more thorough inspections, detect defects in real-time, and streamline their documentation processes. As AI technology continues to advance, the possibilities for enhancing inspection and defect detection in construction are limitless, making it an exciting field for those looking to stay ahead of the curve in the industry.

Ensuring Compliance with Industry Standards

Ensuring compliance with industry standards is crucial when implementing AI applications in construction. These standards are put in place to ensure the safety, quality, and efficiency of construction projects. By adhering to industry standards, construction companies can avoid costly mistakes, delays, and potential legal issues.

One important aspect of compliance with industry standards is ensuring that AI applications in construction meet all safety regulations. This includes ensuring that AI algorithms are accurate and reliable, and that they do not pose any risks to workers or the public. Companies must also ensure that AI applications are compatible with existing safety protocols and procedures on construction sites.

In addition to safety, compliance with industry standards also involves ensuring that AI applications meet quality control measures. This includes monitoring the performance of AI algorithms, ensuring that they are producing accurate results, and making adjustments as needed. Companies must also ensure that AI applications are capable of meeting project requirements and specifications.

Another important aspect of compliance with industry standards is ensuring that AI applications in construction meet all legal and regulatory requirements. This includes ensuring that AI algorithms are compliant with data privacy laws, intellectual property rights, and other legal considerations. Companies must also ensure that they have the proper licenses and permits to use AI applications in construction.

Overall, ensuring compliance with industry standards is essential for the successful implementation of AI applications in construction. By following these standards, companies can ensure that their projects are safe, efficient, and high-quality. Additionally, compliance with industry standards can help companies avoid costly mistakes, delays, and legal issues, ultimately leading to more successful construction projects.

Continuous Improvement in Quality Assurance Processes

Quality assurance is a critical aspect of any construction project, ensuring that the final product meets the required standards and specifications. In the realm of AI applications in construction, quality assurance processes are continuously evolving to incorporate new technologies and methodologies. This subchapter will delve into the various ways in which AI is being utilized to enhance quality assurance in construction projects.

One of the key benefits of using AI in quality assurance processes is the ability to analyze vast amounts of data quickly and accurately. AI algorithms can identify patterns and anomalies in construction materials, equipment, and processes, helping to detect potential issues before they escalate. This proactive approach to quality assurance can prevent costly rework and delays, ultimately saving time and resources.

AI applications in quality assurance also enable real-time monitoring of construction activities, providing project managers with valuable insights into the progress and performance of their teams. By leveraging AI-powered sensors and cameras, construction companies can track the quality of workmanship, adherence to safety protocols, and compliance with regulations. This continuous monitoring helps to identify areas for improvement and implement corrective measures promptly.

Furthermore, AI can streamline the inspection and testing processes in construction projects, reducing the reliance on manual labor and human error. Automated systems powered by AI can conduct quality checks on materials, structures, and installations with precision and efficiency. This not only improves the accuracy of quality assurance but also speeds up the decision-making process, allowing for faster resolution of issues.

In conclusion, continuous improvement in quality assurance processes through AI applications is revolutionizing the construction industry. By harnessing the power of AI algorithms, real-time monitoring systems, and automated inspection technologies, construction companies can ensure that their projects meet the highest standards of quality and safety. As AI continues to advance, the possibilities for enhancing quality assurance in construction are limitless, paving the way for more efficient, cost-effective, and sustainable practices in the built environment.

Chapter 7: AI Applications in Construction Cost Estimation

Accurate Cost Predictions with AI

Accurate cost predictions are essential in the construction industry to ensure projects are completed within budget and on schedule. With the advancement of artificial intelligence (AI) technology, construction professionals now have access to powerful tools that can help improve cost estimation accuracy. AI applications in construction have revolutionized the way cost predictions are made, providing more reliable and precise estimates.

One of the key benefits of using AI for cost predictions in construction is the ability to analyze vast amounts of data quickly and efficiently. AI algorithms can process historical project data, market trends, material costs, labor rates, and other factors to generate accurate cost estimates. By leveraging machine learning and predictive analytics, construction professionals can make informed decisions based on real-time data, reducing the risk of cost overruns and delays.

AI applications in construction also enable project managers to identify potential cost-saving opportunities and optimize resource allocation. By analyzing past project performance and comparing it to current data, AI can help identify areas where costs can be reduced without compromising quality. This proactive approach to cost management can lead to significant savings and improve project profitability.

Furthermore, AI can help construction professionals identify potential risks and uncertainties that may impact project costs. By analyzing historical data and using predictive modeling techniques, AI can forecast potential cost fluctuations and provide recommendations for mitigating risks.

This proactive risk assessment approach can help construction companies better prepare for unexpected events and ensure projects stay on budget.

In conclusion, AI applications in construction have the potential to revolutionize cost estimation practices and improve project outcomes. By leveraging AI technology, construction professionals can make more accurate predictions, optimize resource allocation, identify cost-saving opportunities, and mitigate risks. For those looking to enhance their knowledge of AI applications in construction, understanding how AI can improve cost predictions is essential for success in the industry.

Budget Optimization and Cost Reduction Strategies

Budget optimization and cost reduction strategies are essential components of successful construction projects. By leveraging artificial intelligence (AI) applications in construction, project managers and stakeholders can streamline processes, identify cost-saving opportunities, and maximize the efficiency of their operations. In this subchapter, we will explore various AI tools and technologies that can help construction professionals achieve their budget optimization and cost reduction goals.

One of the key benefits of AI applications in construction is the ability to analyze vast amounts of data in real-time to identify potential cost-saving opportunities. By utilizing machine learning algorithms, construction companies can predict project costs more accurately, optimize resource allocation, and identify areas where costs can be reduced. This proactive approach to cost management can help prevent budget overruns and ensure that projects are completed within the allocated budget.

Another important aspect of budget optimization and cost reduction in construction is the use of AI applications to improve project scheduling and resource management. By implementing AI-driven scheduling tools, construction companies can optimize workflows, reduce downtime, and minimize resource wastage. This not only helps to reduce costs but also improves project timelines and overall efficiency.

AI applications in construction can also help to optimize material management processes, reduce waste, and minimize material costs. By using AI-powered inventory management systems, construction companies can track material usage, monitor inventory levels, and automate orders to ensure that materials are always available when needed. This can lead to significant cost savings and improved project outcomes.

Furthermore, AI applications can be used to monitor equipment performance, identify maintenance needs, and reduce downtime. By implementing predictive maintenance solutions powered by AI, construction companies can prevent costly equipment failures, extend the lifespan of their assets, and reduce maintenance costs. This proactive approach to equipment monitoring can help construction companies optimize their operations and minimize unexpected expenses.

In conclusion, AI applications in construction offer a wide range of opportunities for budget optimization and cost reduction. By leveraging AI tools and technologies, construction professionals can streamline processes, improve project scheduling, optimize material management, monitor equipment performance, and identify cost-saving opportunities. By incorporating AI into their operations, construction companies can achieve greater efficiency, reduce costs, and ensure the success of their projects.

Enhancing Cost Transparency and Accountability

Enhancing cost transparency and accountability is a crucial aspect of utilizing AI applications in construction. By leveraging AI technology, construction companies can gain deeper insights into their cost structures and make more informed decisions to optimize project budgets. This subchapter will explore various ways in which AI can enhance cost transparency and accountability in construction projects.

One key way in which AI can enhance cost transparency is through automated cost estimation tools. These tools use historical data, project specifications, and other relevant factors to generate accurate cost estimates for construction projects. By automating this process, construction companies can reduce the risk of human error and ensure that their cost estimates are as precise as possible.

In addition to automated cost estimation tools, AI can also be used to monitor and track project expenses in real-time. By analyzing data from various sources, such as invoices, receipts, and project reports, AI systems can provide construction companies with a comprehensive view of their current spending and help identify areas where costs can be reduced or optimized.

Furthermore, AI can help improve accountability in construction projects by tracking the performance of subcontractors, suppliers, and other stakeholders. By analyzing data on project timelines, budgets, and deliverables, AI systems can identify patterns of behavior that may indicate potential cost overruns or delays. This information can then be used to hold stakeholders accountable for their performance and ensure that projects stay on track.

Overall, enhancing cost transparency and accountability through AI applications can lead to more efficient and cost-effective construction projects. By leveraging AI technology to automate cost estimation, monitor expenses, and track stakeholder performance, construction companies can make better-informed decisions and ultimately improve their bottom line. This subchapter will delve into the specific tools and strategies that can be used to enhance cost transparency and accountability in construction projects using AI.

Chapter 8: AI Applications in Construction Equipment Monitoring

Predictive Maintenance for Construction Machinery

Predictive maintenance is a crucial aspect of ensuring the longevity and efficiency of construction machinery. By utilizing artificial intelligence (AI) applications in construction, predictive maintenance can be taken to the next level. AI algorithms can analyze data from sensors and historical maintenance records to predict when a piece of machinery is likely to fail. This proactive approach allows construction companies to schedule maintenance before a breakdown occurs, minimizing downtime and reducing repair costs.

One of the key benefits of predictive maintenance for construction machinery is the ability to prevent unexpected breakdowns. Construction projects are often time-sensitive, and any unplanned equipment downtime can lead to costly delays. By using AI applications to predict when maintenance is needed, construction companies can ensure that their machinery is always in optimal working condition, reducing the risk of unexpected failures that can derail a project.

AI applications in construction can also help optimize maintenance schedules for construction machinery. By analyzing data on equipment usage and operating conditions, AI algorithms can recommend the most efficient times for maintenance tasks to be performed. This can help construction companies minimize disruption to their operations while still ensuring that their machinery is properly maintained.

Furthermore, predictive maintenance can help construction companies extend the lifespan of their machinery. By identifying potential issues before they escalate into major problems, AI applications can help prevent premature equipment failures and costly replacements. This can result in significant cost savings for construction companies in the long run, as well as improved operational efficiency.

In conclusion, predictive maintenance for construction machinery is an essential application of AI in the construction industry. By leveraging AI algorithms to analyze data and predict maintenance needs, construction companies can improve equipment reliability, reduce downtime, and optimize maintenance schedules. With the potential to extend the lifespan of machinery and minimize repair costs, predictive maintenance is a valuable tool for any construction company looking to maximize the efficiency and productivity of their operations.

Real-time Tracking and Monitoring of Equipment Performance

Real-time tracking and monitoring of equipment performance is a crucial aspect of construction projects, as it allows project managers to optimize productivity, ensure safety, and minimize downtime. With the advent of artificial intelligence (AI) technologies, tracking and monitoring equipment performance has become more efficient and accurate than ever before. In this subchapter, we will explore the various ways in which AI is revolutionizing equipment monitoring in the construction industry.

One of the key benefits of real-time tracking and monitoring of equipment performance using AI is the ability to predict and prevent potential issues before they escalate. AI algorithms can analyze data from sensors and other sources to identify patterns and anomalies that may indicate a problem with a piece of equipment. By detecting issues early on, project managers can schedule preventive maintenance to avoid costly breakdowns and delays.

Another advantage of AI-powered equipment monitoring is the ability to optimize equipment usage and reduce energy consumption. AI algorithms can analyze equipment performance data in real-time to identify inefficiencies and suggest ways to improve utilization. For example, AI can recommend optimal operating parameters for equipment based on current conditions, such as weather and workload, to minimize energy waste and extend the lifespan of the equipment.

Furthermore, AI can help construction companies improve safety on job sites by monitoring equipment performance and alerting workers to potential hazards. For example, AI can detect abnormal vibrations in a crane or excavator that may indicate a mechanical issue, prompting workers to evacuate the area before a catastrophic failure occurs. By providing real-time insights into equipment performance, AI can help prevent accidents and injuries on construction sites.

In conclusion, real-time tracking and monitoring of equipment performance using AI is revolutionizing the construction industry by enabling project managers to optimize productivity, ensure safety, and minimize downtime. By leveraging AI technologies, construction companies can predict and prevent equipment failures, optimize energy usage, and improve safety on job sites. As AI continues to advance, we can expect even greater innovations in equipment monitoring that will further enhance the efficiency and effectiveness of construction projects.

Improving Equipment Utilization and Efficiency with AI

In the construction industry, equipment plays a crucial role in completing projects efficiently and on time. However, managing equipment utilization and ensuring efficiency can be challenging. This is where Artificial Intelligence (AI) comes into play, offering innovative solutions to improve equipment performance and productivity. By harnessing the power of AI, construction companies can optimize their equipment usage, reduce downtime, and ultimately increase profitability.

One of the key ways AI can enhance equipment utilization is through predictive maintenance. By analyzing data from sensors and equipment monitoring systems, AI algorithms can predict when maintenance is needed before a breakdown occurs. This proactive approach not only minimizes downtime but also extends the lifespan of equipment, saving companies time and money in the long run.

Another way AI can improve equipment efficiency is through real-time monitoring and optimization. By using AI-powered systems to track equipment usage and performance, construction companies can identify inefficiencies and make adjustments to maximize output. For example, AI can analyze data to determine the best times to schedule maintenance or optimize equipment settings for optimal performance.

AI can also assist in equipment scheduling and allocation. By analyzing project timelines, resource availability, and equipment capabilities, AI algorithms can recommend the most efficient use of equipment to meet project deadlines. This ensures that equipment is utilized to its full potential, reducing idle time and maximizing productivity.

Furthermore, AI can enhance equipment safety by monitoring usage patterns and detecting potential hazards. By analyzing data in real-time, AI systems can alert operators to unsafe conditions or potential risks, helping to prevent accidents and injuries on the job site. This proactive approach to safety not only protects workers but also minimizes equipment downtime due to accidents.

Overall, AI offers a wide range of benefits for improving equipment utilization and efficiency in the construction industry. By leveraging AI-powered solutions, companies can optimize equipment performance, reduce downtime, enhance safety, and ultimately increase profitability. As technology continues to advance, the role of AI in construction equipment management will only become more essential for companies looking to stay competitive in the industry.

Chapter 9: AI Applications in Construction Risk Assessment

Identifying and Analyzing Potential Risks Using AI

In the construction industry, identifying and analyzing potential risks is crucial to ensure projects are completed safely, on time, and within budget. With the advancement of artificial intelligence (AI) technology, construction professionals now have powerful tools at their disposal to streamline the risk assessment process. AI can help identify potential risks, analyze their impact, and provide insights to mitigate these risks effectively.

One of the key benefits of using AI in risk assessment is its ability to process vast amounts of data quickly and accurately. By analyzing historical project data, AI algorithms can identify patterns and trends that may indicate potential risks in current projects. This predictive analysis can help construction professionals proactively address issues before they escalate, saving time and resources in the long run.

AI applications in risk assessment can also enhance decision-making processes by providing real-time insights into potential risks. By combining data from sensors, drones, and other monitoring technologies, AI systems can detect safety hazards, structural vulnerabilities, and other risks in real-time. This allows construction teams to take immediate action to mitigate risks and prevent accidents before they occur.

Furthermore, AI can help construction professionals prioritize risks based on their impact and likelihood of occurrence. By using machine learning algorithms, AI systems can assign risk scores to different scenarios, helping teams focus their resources on the most critical issues. This targeted approach can improve project outcomes and minimize the potential for costly delays and disruptions.

Overall, AI applications in risk assessment offer construction professionals a powerful tool for identifying, analyzing, and mitigating potential risks. By leveraging AI technology, construction teams can improve project safety, efficiency, and overall success. As AI continues to evolve, its role in risk assessment in the construction industry will only become more essential in ensuring projects are completed successfully.

Developing Risk Mitigation Strategies with Artificial Intelligence

Developing risk mitigation strategies is a crucial aspect of any construction project, as unforeseen events can lead to costly delays and safety hazards. With the advancement of artificial intelligence (AI) technology, construction professionals now have powerful tools at their disposal to proactively manage risks and ensure project success. In this subchapter, we will explore how AI can be utilized to develop effective risk mitigation strategies in construction projects.

One key benefit of using AI in risk mitigation is its ability to analyze large datasets and identify potential risks before they escalate. By leveraging machine learning algorithms, AI can process vast amounts of project data, including historical records, weather patterns, and site conditions, to predict potential risks and recommend mitigation strategies. This proactive approach allows project managers to address risks early on and prevent costly setbacks.

AI can also be used to automate risk assessment processes, saving time and reducing human error. Through the use of AI-powered risk assessment tools, construction professionals can quickly identify high-risk areas and prioritize mitigation efforts. This real-time analysis enables project teams to make informed decisions and allocate resources effectively to minimize risks throughout the project lifecycle.

Furthermore, AI can enhance decision-making by providing real-time insights and recommendations based on current project conditions. By incorporating AI into risk management processes, construction professionals can access valuable information that can help them make more informed decisions and adapt quickly to changing circumstances. This agility is essential in mitigating risks and ensuring project success in the dynamic construction environment.

In addition to risk assessment and decision support, AI can also be used to optimize risk mitigation strategies by simulating potential scenarios and evaluating the effectiveness of different mitigation measures. Through AI-driven simulations, project teams can test various risk mitigation strategies in a virtual environment, allowing them to identify the most effective approaches and refine their plans before implementation. This iterative process can significantly improve the overall effectiveness of risk mitigation efforts and enhance project outcomes.

In conclusion, the integration of AI technology in risk mitigation strategies offers construction professionals a powerful tool to proactively manage risks, make informed decisions, and optimize mitigation efforts. By leveraging AI capabilities, project teams can identify potential risks early, automate risk assessment processes, enhance decision-making, and simulate different scenarios to develop effective risk mitigation strategies. Embracing AI applications in risk management can help construction projects mitigate risks, ensure safety, and achieve successful outcomes in an increasingly complex and competitive industry.

Enhancing Project Resilience and Preparedness through AI

In the realm of construction projects, resilience and preparedness are key factors that can make or break the success of a venture. With the advancement of technology, Artificial Intelligence (AI) has emerged as a powerful tool that can enhance project resilience and preparedness in numerous ways. In this subchapter, we will explore how AI applications can be utilized to strengthen construction projects and ensure their success.

AI applications in construction safety play a crucial role in enhancing project resilience and preparedness. By utilizing AI-powered sensors and cameras, construction sites can be monitored in real-time to identify potential safety hazards and prevent accidents before they occur. AI algorithms can analyze data to predict potential risks and provide recommendations for improving safety protocols. This proactive approach to safety not only protects workers but also minimizes project delays and costs associated with accidents.

In the realm of project management, AI applications offer valuable insights that can help enhance resilience and preparedness. AI algorithms can analyze vast amounts of data to identify patterns and trends, allowing project managers to make more informed decisions. By utilizing AI-powered project management tools, construction projects can be better planned, executed, and monitored, leading to improved efficiency and reduced risks of delays or cost overruns.

AI applications in construction materials management also play a significant role in enhancing project resilience and preparedness. By utilizing AI-powered inventory management systems, construction companies can optimize their supply chain, ensuring that materials are available when needed and minimizing delays. AI algorithms can predict material shortages or surpluses, allowing project managers to make adjustments in real-time to prevent disruptions.

In the realm of construction scheduling, AI applications offer valuable tools that can enhance project resilience and preparedness. By utilizing AI algorithms, construction schedules can be optimized to account for potential risks and uncertainties. AI-powered scheduling tools can identify critical path activities and provide recommendations for mitigating potential delays. This proactive approach to scheduling ensures that projects stay on track and are completed on time.

In conclusion, AI applications offer a wide range of tools and technologies that can enhance project resilience and preparedness in the construction industry. By utilizing AI-powered solutions in safety, project management, materials management, and scheduling, construction companies can improve efficiency, reduce risks, and ensure the success of their projects. For anyone looking to learn more about AI applications in construction and how they can be utilized to enhance project resilience and preparedness, this subchapter provides a comprehensive overview of the topic.

Chapter 10: AI Applications in Sustainable Construction Practices using AI

Implementing Green Building Solutions with AI

Implementing green building solutions with AI is an essential aspect of modern construction practices. By incorporating artificial intelligence technologies into building projects, construction companies can greatly reduce their environmental impact and create more sustainable structures. AI can be used to optimize energy usage, reduce waste, and improve overall efficiency in the construction process.

One of the key ways AI can help implement green building solutions is through energy management. AI algorithms can analyze data from sensors and meters to optimize energy usage in buildings, reducing overall consumption and costs. This can lead to significant reductions in carbon emissions and help buildings achieve higher energy efficiency ratings.

AI can also be used to improve waste management practices in construction projects. By analyzing data on waste generation and disposal, AI can identify patterns and trends to help companies minimize waste and recycle materials more effectively. This not only reduces the environmental impact of construction projects but also saves money in the long run.

Another important application of AI in green building solutions is in materials management. AI can help construction companies source sustainable materials, track their usage, and optimize their procurement processes. By using AI to analyze data on materials usage and availability, companies can make more informed decisions that promote sustainable practices.

In conclusion, implementing green building solutions with AI is a crucial step towards creating more sustainable and environmentally-friendly construction practices. By harnessing the power of artificial intelligence, construction companies can reduce their environmental impact, improve energy efficiency, and create more sustainable structures for the future. It is essential for anyone interested in AI applications in construction to understand the importance of incorporating green building solutions into their projects.

Energy Efficiency Optimization in Construction Projects

Energy efficiency optimization in construction projects is a crucial aspect of modern construction practices, as the industry strives to reduce its environmental impact and operating costs. By incorporating artificial intelligence (AI) applications into construction projects, contractors can achieve significant energy savings and improve overall project efficiency. In this subchapter, we will explore the various ways in which AI can be used to optimize energy efficiency in construction projects.

One of the key areas where AI can make a significant impact on energy efficiency in construction projects is in the design phase. AI algorithms can analyze building designs and recommend energy-efficient solutions, such as optimal building orientation, window placement, and insulation materials. By leveraging AI technology, architects and engineers can create buildings that consume less energy and require fewer resources to maintain optimal indoor conditions.

In addition to design optimization, AI can also be used to monitor and control energy usage in construction projects. Smart building systems equipped with AI technology can automatically adjust heating, cooling, and lighting levels based on occupancy patterns and environmental conditions. This real-time monitoring and control system ensures that energy is used efficiently and minimizes waste, leading to lower operating costs and reduced environmental impact.

Furthermore, AI applications can help construction project managers make informed decisions that optimize energy efficiency throughout the project lifecycle. By analyzing data from sensors and other sources, AI algorithms can identify areas of inefficiency and recommend strategies for improvement. This proactive approach to energy management can result in significant cost savings and environmental benefits, making construction projects more sustainable and competitive in the market.

Overall, energy efficiency optimization in construction projects is a complex and multifaceted challenge that can be effectively addressed with the help of AI applications. By leveraging AI technology in design, monitoring, and decision-making processes, construction companies can achieve significant improvements in energy efficiency, reduce operating costs, and enhance their sustainability credentials. This subchapter serves as a comprehensive guide to understanding the potential of AI in optimizing energy efficiency in construction projects, providing valuable insights and practical strategies for implementation.

Promoting Environmental Sustainability through AI-driven Practices

Promoting environmental sustainability through AI-driven practices is becoming increasingly important in the construction industry. By harnessing the power of artificial intelligence, construction companies can reduce their carbon footprint, minimize waste, and optimize resource usage. AI applications in construction offer innovative solutions that can help mitigate the environmental impact of building projects.

One key way AI can promote environmental sustainability in construction is through the optimization of construction materials management. By utilizing AI algorithms, companies can better track and manage their materials, reducing waste and minimizing the need for excessive production. This not only helps reduce costs but also contributes to a more sustainable construction process overall.

AI applications in construction scheduling also play a crucial role in promoting environmental sustainability. By optimizing project timelines and resources, AI can help minimize energy consumption and reduce greenhouse gas emissions. This can lead to more efficient construction practices that are not only cost-effective but also environmentally friendly.

In addition, AI-driven practices can enhance construction site optimization by analyzing data to improve workflows and reduce inefficiencies. By utilizing AI technologies, companies can optimize site layouts, improve traffic flow, and reduce energy usage. This can lead to a more sustainable construction site that minimizes its impact on the environment.

Overall, the integration of AI applications in construction can significantly contribute to promoting environmental sustainability in the industry. By leveraging AI-driven practices in materials management, scheduling, and site optimization, construction companies can minimize waste, reduce energy consumption, and improve overall efficiency. As the construction industry continues to evolve, embracing AI technologies will be essential in creating a more sustainable future for our planet.

Chapter 11: AI Applications in Construction Site Optimization

Maximizing Site Layout Efficiency with AI

In the construction industry, maximizing site layout efficiency is key to ensuring projects are completed on time and within budget. With the advancements in artificial intelligence (AI) technology, construction companies now have powerful tools at their disposal to help streamline their processes and improve overall efficiency. This subchapter will explore how AI can be used to optimize site layout and maximize efficiency in construction projects.

One of the ways AI can help maximize site layout efficiency is through the use of predictive analytics. By analyzing historical data and real-time information, AI algorithms can predict potential bottlenecks and inefficiencies in the site layout. This allows construction managers to make informed decisions and adjustments to the layout before issues arise, saving time and resources in the long run.

Another way AI can improve site layout efficiency is through the use of autonomous drones and robots. These AI-powered devices can survey construction sites, gather data, and even assist in the layout process. By automating certain tasks, construction companies can free up valuable human resources to focus on more complex and critical aspects of the project, ultimately speeding up the construction timeline.

AI can also be used to optimize material delivery and storage on construction sites. By analyzing data on material usage, AI algorithms can help construction managers determine the most efficient way to store and distribute materials, reducing waste and minimizing delays. This not only improves site layout efficiency but also contributes to overall cost savings for the project.

Furthermore, AI can assist in real-time monitoring of equipment and resources on construction sites. By using sensors and IoT technology, AI algorithms can track the location and status of equipment, predict maintenance needs, and even optimize equipment usage to prevent downtime. This proactive approach to equipment monitoring can help construction companies maximize efficiency and productivity on site.

Overall, AI has the potential to revolutionize the construction industry by maximizing site layout efficiency and improving project outcomes. By leveraging AI technologies in predictive analytics, autonomous devices, material management, and equipment monitoring, construction companies can streamline their processes, reduce costs, and deliver projects more efficiently. As the technology continues to advance, the possibilities for optimizing construction site layouts with AI are endless.

Traffic Management and Logistics Optimization Using Artificial Intelligence

Traffic management and logistics optimization are crucial aspects of construction projects, as they directly impact project timelines, costs, and overall efficiency. Thanks to advancements in artificial intelligence (AI), construction companies can now leverage cutting-edge technology to streamline traffic management and logistics operations. By harnessing AI algorithms and machine learning capabilities, construction firms can effectively optimize their transportation networks, reduce congestion, and enhance overall project delivery.

One of the key benefits of using AI for traffic management and logistics optimization in construction is the ability to predict and mitigate potential bottlenecks before they occur. By analyzing historical data, real-time traffic patterns, and weather conditions, AI systems can proactively identify areas of congestion and recommend alternative routes or scheduling adjustments to ensure smooth transportation flow. This predictive capability not only helps minimize delays and disruptions but also enhances safety for workers and equipment on the job site.

Furthermore, AI applications in traffic management and logistics optimization can help construction companies optimize their fleet management processes. By integrating AI-powered telematics systems into their vehicles, firms can track and monitor the real-time location, performance, and maintenance needs of their fleet. This level of visibility allows project managers to make informed decisions regarding vehicle routing, fuel efficiency, and maintenance scheduling, ultimately reducing costs and improving overall operational efficiency.

In addition to fleet management, AI can also be used to optimize material delivery schedules and inventory management. By analyzing historical data, supply chain trends, and project timelines, AI systems can generate accurate demand forecasts and optimize delivery routes to ensure that materials are delivered to the job site exactly when they are needed. This level of precision not only reduces waste and inventory holding costs but also improves overall project productivity and profitability.

Overall, the integration of AI applications in traffic management and logistics optimization represents a significant opportunity for construction companies to enhance their operational efficiency, reduce costs, and improve project outcomes. By leveraging AI algorithms and machine learning capabilities, firms can proactively address traffic congestion, optimize fleet management, and streamline material delivery processes. As the construction industry continues to embrace digital transformation, AI will play a pivotal role in driving innovation and efficiency across all aspects of project delivery.

Enhancing Productivity and Safety on Construction Sites through AI Integration

In today's rapidly evolving construction industry, the integration of artificial intelligence (AI) technologies is revolutionizing the way projects are planned, executed, and managed. One of the key areas where AI is making a significant impact is in enhancing productivity and safety on construction sites. By harnessing the power of AI, construction companies can streamline their operations, minimize risks, and ultimately improve project outcomes.

AI applications in construction safety play a crucial role in preventing accidents and ensuring the well-being of workers on site. Through the use of sensors, drones, and other advanced technologies, AI can monitor and analyze data in real-time to identify potential safety hazards. By proactively addressing these risks, construction companies can create a safer work environment and reduce the likelihood of accidents occurring. This not only protects the health and safety of workers but also helps companies avoid costly delays and liabilities.

In addition to safety, AI applications in construction project management can help companies optimize their workflows and improve efficiency. By analyzing historical data and project performance metrics, AI can provide valuable insights into areas where processes can be streamlined and resources can be allocated more effectively. This allows construction companies to identify bottlenecks, prioritize tasks, and make data-driven decisions that enhance productivity and project outcomes.

Furthermore, AI applications in construction materials management can help companies better track and manage the flow of materials on site. By using AI-powered inventory management systems, construction companies can optimize their supply chain, reduce waste, and ensure that materials are delivered to the right place at the right time. This not only improves efficiency but also helps companies save time and money by minimizing delays and disruptions caused by material shortages or mismanagement.

Overall, the integration of AI technologies in construction is transforming the way projects are executed and managed. By leveraging AI applications in safety, project management, materials management, and other key areas, construction companies can enhance productivity, reduce risks, and ultimately achieve better project outcomes. For anyone looking to learn more about how AI is reshaping the construction industry, this comprehensive guide provides valuable insights and practical advice on how to leverage AI to optimize construction site operations.

Conclusion: The Future of AI in Construction and Beyond

In conclusion, the future of AI in construction is incredibly promising and full of potential. As we have explored throughout this guide, AI applications in construction have the ability to revolutionize the industry in numerous ways. From improving safety and project management to optimizing construction sites and reducing costs, AI has the power to transform the way we build.

One of the key areas where AI will continue to make an impact is in construction safety. By using AI-powered tools to monitor and analyze data, construction companies can identify potential hazards and risks before they become accidents. This proactive approach to safety can help prevent injuries and save lives on construction sites.

Additionally, AI applications in construction project management will streamline processes and improve efficiency. By automating tasks and providing real-time insights, project managers can make better decisions and keep projects on track. This will ultimately lead to faster completion times and higher quality outcomes.

In terms of materials management, AI can help construction companies optimize inventory levels, reduce waste, and lower costs. By using predictive analytics and machine learning algorithms, companies can better forecast material needs and ensure they have the right supplies on hand when they are needed.

Overall, the future of AI in construction is bright. As technology continues to advance and new innovations are developed, we can expect to see even greater improvements in safety, project management, materials management, scheduling, quality control, cost estimation, equipment monitoring, risk assessment, sustainable practices, and construction site optimization. By embracing AI applications in construction, companies can stay ahead of the curve and lead the industry into a more efficient and sustainable future.

www.ingramcontent.com/pod-product-compliance
Lightning Source LLC
LaVergne TN
LVHW081808050326
832903LV00027B/2143

9798324596132